Sunday
Suppers
Classic Recipes™

Publications International, Ltd.
Favorite Brand Name Recipes at www.fbnr.com

Pictured on the front cover: Herb Roasted Turkey (page 29).

ISBN: 1-4127-0433-2

Library of Congress Catalog Card Number: 00-109777

Manufactured in China.

8 7 6 5 4 3 2 1

Microwave Cooking: Microwave ovens vary in wattage. Use the cooking times as guidelines and check for doneness before adding more time.

Preparation/Cooking Times: Preparation times are based on the approximate amount of time required to assemble the recipe before cooking, baking, chilling or serving. These times include preparation steps such as measuring, chopping and mixing. The fact that some preparations and cooking can be done simultaneously is taken into account. Preparation of optional ingredients and serving suggestions is not included.

Table of Contents

Soups, Stews & Breads

Nothing says Sunday supper like a steaming bowl of homemade soup and a loaf of fresh-baked bread. From Beef Barley to Chicken Noodle, there's something for everyone.

Beef Barley Soup

$^1/_2$ pound ground beef

$2^1/_2$ cups water

1 can ($14^1/_2$ ounces) stewed tomatoes, cut up

3 medium carrots, sliced

$^3/_4$ cup sliced mushrooms

$^1/_2$ cup quick barley, uncooked

2 cloves garlic, minced

1 teaspoon dried oregano leaves, crushed

$^1/_2$ pound (8 ounces) VELVEETA® Pasteurized Prepared Cheese
    Product, cut up

Salt and pepper

1. Brown meat in large saucepan; drain. Stir in water, tomatoes, carrots, mushrooms, barley, garlic and oregano.

2. Bring to boil. Reduce heat to low; cover. Simmer 10 minutes or until barley is tender.

3. Add Velveeta; stir until melted. Season to taste with salt and pepper.

Makes 6 (1-cup) servings

Prep Time: 15 minutes
Cook Time: 20 minutes

Crispy Onion Crescent Rolls

1 can (8 ounces) refrigerated crescent dinner rolls
1¹/₃ cups *French's*® *Taste Toppers*™ French Fried Onions, slightly
   crushed
1 egg, beaten

Preheat oven to 375°F. Line large baking sheet with foil. Separate
refrigerated rolls into 8 triangles. Sprinkle center of each triangle with
about 1¹/₂ tablespoons *Taste Toppers*. Roll up triangles from short side,
jelly-roll fashion. Sprinkle any excess *Taste Toppers* over top of crescents.

Arrange crescents on prepared baking sheet. Brush with beaten egg. Bake
15 minutes or until golden brown and crispy. Transfer to wire rack; cool
slightly. *Makes 8 servings*

Lentil Soup

1 tablespoon FILIPPO BERIO® Olive Oil
1 medium onion, diced
4 cups beef broth
1 cup dried lentils, rinsed and drained
¹/₄ cup tomato sauce
1 teaspoon dried Italian herb seasoning
   Salt and freshly ground black pepper

In large saucepan, heat olive oil over medium heat until hot. Add onion;
cook and stir 5 minutes or until softened. Add beef broth; bring mixture
to a boil. Stir in lentils, tomato sauce and Italian seasoning. Cover; reduce
heat to low and simmer 45 minutes or until lentils are tender. Season to
taste with salt and pepper. Serve hot. *Makes 6 servings*

Crispy Onion Crescent Rolls

Skillet Sausage and Bean Stew

1 pound spicy Italian sausage, casing removed and sliced $1/2$ inch thick

$1/2$ onion, chopped

2 cups frozen O'Brien-style potatoes with onions and peppers

1 can (15 ounces) pinto beans, undrained

$3/4$ cup water

1 teaspoon beef bouillon granules *or* 1 beef bouillon cube

1 teaspoon dried oregano leaves

$1/8$ teaspoon ground red pepper

1. Combine sausage slices and onion in large nonstick skillet; cook and stir over medium-high heat 5 to 7 minutes or until meat is no longer pink. Drain drippings.

2. Stir in potatoes, beans, water, bouillon, oregano and red pepper; reduce heat to medium. Cover and simmer 15 minutes, stirring occasionally.

Makes 4 servings

Tip: You can reduce the calories and fat content of this dish by substituting turkey sausage for Italian sausage. Add hot pepper sauce to taste if you prefer a spicier stew.

Prep and Cook Time: 30 minutes

Skillet Sausage and Bean Stew

Veg•All® Beef Chili

1 can (28 ounces) tomato sauce

1 pound ground beef, browned and drained

1 can (16 ounces) kidney beans, drained and rinsed

1 can (15 ounces) VEG•ALL® Original Mixed Vegetables, with liquid

1 can (14½ ounces) whole tomatoes, cut up

¾ cup sliced green onions

2 teaspoons chili powder

¼ teaspoon black pepper

Corn chips

Shredded cheese

Diced green onions

In 3-quart saucepan, combine all ingredients. Bring to a boil; reduce heat, cover, and simmer for 20 to 30 minutes, stirring occasionally. Serve hot with corn chips, shredded cheese and diced green onions as toppers.

Makes 6 to 8 servings

Note: A vegetarian version can be made by eliminating the ground beef and adding 1 teaspoon dried oregano and ½ teaspoon ground cumin.

Prep Time: 7 minutes
Cook Time: 20 minutes

Campbell's® Hearty Chicken Noodle Soup

2 cans (10$\frac{1}{2}$ ounces each) CAMPBELL'S® Condensed
    Chicken Broth
1 cup water
    Generous dash pepper
1 medium carrot, sliced (about $\frac{1}{2}$ cup)
1 stalk celery, sliced (about $\frac{1}{2}$ cup)
2 skinless, boneless chicken breast halves, cut up
$\frac{1}{2}$ cup *uncooked* medium egg noodles

1. In medium saucepan mix broth, water, pepper, carrot, celery and chicken. Over medium-high heat, heat to a boil.

2. Stir in noodles. Reduce heat to medium. Cook 10 minutes or until noodles are done, stirring often.   *Makes 4 servings*

Tip: Save time by using precut carrots and celery from your supermarket salad bar.

Prep/Cook Time: 20 minutes

13

Hearty Tortellini Soup

1 small red onion, chopped

2 medium carrots, chopped

2 ribs celery, thinly sliced

1 small zucchini, chopped

2 plum tomatoes, chopped

2 cloves garlic, minced

2 cans (14½ ounces *each*) chicken broth

1 can (15 to 19 ounces) red kidney beans, rinsed and drained

2 tablespoons *French's® Worcestershire Sauce*

1 package (9 ounces) refrigerated tortellini pasta

1. Heat *2 tablespoons oil* in 6-quart saucepot or Dutch oven over medium-high heat. Add vegetables, tomatoes and garlic. Cook and stir 5 minutes or until vegetables are crisp-tender.

2. Add broth, *½ cup water,* beans and Worcestershire. Heat to boiling. Stir in pasta. Return to boiling. Cook 5 minutes or until pasta is tender, stirring occasionally. Serve with crusty bread and grated Parmesan cheese, if desired.   *Makes 4 servings*

Prep Time: 15 minutes
Cook Time: 10 minutes

Hearty Tortellini Soup

Irish Soda Bread

    4 cups all-purpose flour
$^1/_4$ cup sugar
    1 tablespoon baking powder
    1 teaspoon baking soda
    1 teaspoon salt
    1 tablespoon caraway seeds
$^1/_3$ cup vegetable shortening
    1 cup raisins or currants
    1 egg
$1^3/_4$ cups buttermilk*

Or, substitute soured fresh milk. To sour milk, place 2 tablespoons lemon juice plus enough milk to equal $1^3/_4$ cups in 2-cup measure. Stir; let stand 5 minutes before using.

1. Preheat oven to 350°F. Grease large baking sheet; set aside.

2. Sift flour, sugar, baking powder, baking soda and salt into large bowl. Stir in caraway seeds. Cut in shortening with pastry blender or 2 knives until mixture resembles coarse crumbs. Stir in raisins. Beat egg in medium bowl using fork. Add buttermilk; beat until well combined. Add buttermilk mixture to flour mixture; stir until mixture forms soft dough that clings together and forms a ball.

3. Turn dough out onto well-floured surface. Knead dough gently 10 to 12 times. Place dough on prepared baking sheet. Pat dough into 7-inch round. Score top of dough with tip of sharp knife, making an "x" about 4 inches long and $^1/_4$ inch deep.

4. Bake 55 to 60 minutes or until toothpick inserted in center comes out clean. Immediately remove from baking sheet; cool on wire rack. Bread is best eaten the day it is made.   *Makes 12 servings*

Irish Soda Bread

Chicken & White Bean Stew

1 tablespoon olive or vegetable oil

4 medium carrots, sliced (about 2 cups)

3 ribs celery, chopped (about 1 cup)

1 medium onion, thinly sliced

2 cloves garlic, finely chopped

1 pound boneless, skinless chicken breast halves or thighs, cut
  into chunks

1 jar (26 to 28 ounces) RAGÚ® Old World Style® Pasta Sauce

2 cans (15 ounces each) cannellini or white kidney beans, rinsed
  and drained

Pinch crushed red pepper flakes (optional)

In 12-inch skillet, heat oil over medium heat and cook carrots, celery, onion and garlic, stirring occasionally, 5 minutes or until vegetables are tender. Remove vegetables and set aside.

In same skillet, thoroughly brown chicken over medium-high heat. Return vegetables to skillet. Stir in Ragú® Old World Style Pasta Sauce, beans and red pepper flakes. Bring to a boil over high heat. Reduce heat to medium and simmer covered, stirring occasionally, 15 minutes or until chicken is no longer pink. Garnish, if desired, with fresh parsley and serve with toasted Italian bread. *Makes 6 servings*

Country Stew

2 bags SUCCESS® Brown Rice

1 pound ground turkey

1 small onion, chopped

2 cans (14$^1/_2$ ounces each) tomatoes, cut-up, undrained

1 teaspoon pepper

$^1/_2$ teaspoon dried basil leaves, crushed

$^1/_2$ teaspoon garlic powder

1 can (16 ounces) whole kernel corn, drained

Prepare rice according to package directions.

Brown ground turkey with onion in large skillet, stirring occasionally to separate turkey. Add tomatoes, pepper, basil and garlic powder; simmer 20 minutes, stirring occasionally. Stir in rice and corn; heat thoroughly, stirring occasionally. Garnish, if desired.   *Makes 8 servings*

Brown rice is more nutritious than white rice because it contains the bran and germ of the rice kernel. (These are removed during milling to produce white rice.)

Buttermilk Corn Bread Loaf

1 1/2 cups all-purpose flour

1 cup yellow cornmeal

1/3 cup sugar

2 teaspoons baking powder

1 teaspoon salt

1/2 teaspoon baking soda

1/2 cup vegetable shortening

1 1/3 cups buttermilk*

2 eggs

*Or, substitute soured fresh milk. To sour milk, place 4 teaspoons lemon juice plus enough milk to equal 1 1/3 cups in 2-cup measure. Stir; let stand 5 minutes before using.

1. Preheat oven to 375°F. Grease 8 1/2 × 4 1/2-inch loaf pan; set aside.

2. Combine flour, cornmeal, sugar, baking powder, salt and baking soda in medium bowl. Cut in shortening with pastry blender or 2 knives until mixture resembles coarse crumbs.

3. Whisk together buttermilk and eggs in small bowl. Make well in center of dry ingredients. Add buttermilk mixture; stir until mixture forms stiff batter. (Batter will be lumpy.) Turn into prepared pan; spread mixture evenly, removing any air bubbles.

4. Bake 50 to 55 minutes or until toothpick inserted in center comes out clean. Cool in pan on wire rack 10 minutes. Remove from pan; cool on rack 10 minutes more. Serve warm.   *Makes 1 loaf*

Buttermilk Corn Bread Loaf

Country Recipe Biscuits

    2 cups all-purpose flour
    1 tablespoon baking powder
    ½ cup prepared HIDDEN VALLEY® Original Ranch® salad
        dressing
    ½ cup buttermilk

Preheat oven to 425°F. In small bowl, sift together flour and baking powder. Make a well in flour mixture; add salad dressing and buttermilk. Stir with fork until dough forms a ball. Drop by rounded spoonfuls onto ungreased baking sheet. Bake until lightly browned, 12 to 15 minutes.

Makes 12 biscuits

Crowd–Pleasing Poultry

Who can resist a heaping platter of fried chicken or mouthwatering turkey and biscuits? Roasted, baked, broiled or fried, chicken and turkey are family favorites any day of the week—especially on Sunday!

Chicken Rustigo

4 boneless skinless chicken breast halves

1 package (10 ounces) fresh mushrooms, sliced

³/₄ cup chicken broth

¹/₄ cup dry red wine or water

3 tablespoons *French's*® Hearty Deli Brown Mustard

2 medium tomatoes, seeded and coarsely chopped

1 can (14 ounces) artichoke hearts, drained and quartered

2 teaspoons cornstarch

1. Season chicken with salt and pepper. Heat *1 tablespoon oil* in large nonstick skillet over medium-high heat. Cook chicken 5 minutes or until browned on both sides. Remove and set aside.

2. Heat *1 tablespoon oil* in same skillet until hot. Add mushrooms. Cook and stir 5 minutes or until mushrooms are tender. Stir in broth, wine and mustard. Return chicken to skillet. Add tomatoes and artichoke hearts. Heat to boiling. Reduce heat to medium-low. Cook, covered, 10 minutes or until chicken is no longer pink in center.

3. Combine cornstarch with *1 tablespoon cold water*. Stir into skillet. Heat to boiling. Cook, stirring, over high heat about 1 minute or until sauce thickens. Serve with orzo pasta, if desired. *Makes 4 servings*

Prep Time: 10 minutes
Cook Time: 21 minutes

Turkey and Biscuits

2 cans (10³/₄ ounces each) condensed cream of chicken soup,
  undiluted
¹/₄ cup dry white wine
¹/₄ teaspoon poultry seasoning
2 packages (8 ounces each) frozen cut asparagus, thawed
3 cups cubed cooked turkey or chicken
  Paprika (optional)
1 can (11 ounces) refrigerated flaky biscuits

Preheat oven to 350°F. Spray 13×9-inch baking dish with nonstick cooking spray.

Combine soup, wine and poultry seasoning in medium bowl.

Arrange asparagus in single layer in prepared dish. Place turkey evenly over asparagus. Spread soup mixture over turkey. Sprinkle lightly with paprika, if desired.

Cover tightly with foil and bake 20 minutes. Remove from oven. Increase oven temperature to 425°F. Top with biscuits and bake, uncovered, 8 to 10 minutes or until biscuits are golden brown.   *Makes 6 servings*

Turkey and Biscuits

Chicken and Sausage Fettuccine

1 (12-ounce) package BOB EVANS® Original Links
1 boneless, skinless chicken breast, thinly sliced
1 tablespoon olive oil
1 small zucchini, quartered and sliced
4 medium mushrooms, sliced
3 green onions, sliced
1 (12-ounce) package uncooked fettucini
1/2 cup butter or margarine
1/2 cup milk
1/4 cup Parmesan cheese
1 teaspoon garlic powder
1 teaspoon hot pepper sauce
Salt and black pepper to taste

Cook sausage in large skillet until browned. Remove from skillet and cut into 1/2-inch slices. Add chicken to skillet; cook in sausage drippings until no longer pink. Remove and set aside. Heat olive oil in skillet; add zucchini, mushrooms and green onions and cook until crisp-tender. Cook fettucini in large saucepan according to package directions; drain and return to saucepan. Add butter and milk; toss gently until evenly coated. Add sausage, chicken, vegetable mixture, cheese, garlic powder and hot pepper sauce; cook over low heat, tossing gently until well blended and heated through. Add salt and black pepper to taste. Refrigerate leftovers.

Makes 6 servings

Chicken and Sausage Fettuccine

Turkey à la King

2 cups cubed BUTTERBALL® Fat Free Slice 'N Serve Oven
Roasted Breast of Turkey, cubed

$1/3$ cup butter

4 ounces fresh mushrooms, sliced

4 tablespoons flour

$1/2$ teaspoon salt

$1/8$ teaspoon black pepper

1 can ($14^{1}/_2$ ounces) chicken broth

$1/2$ cup light cream

1 cup frozen peas and carrots

Chopped fresh parsley

Melt butter in large saucepan over medium heat; add mushrooms. Cook and stir 5 minutes. Stir in flour, salt and pepper. Slowly blend in chicken broth and cream. Cook, stirring constantly, until thickened. Add turkey and peas and carrots. Heat well. Serve on toasted thick bread slices or pastry shells, if desired. Sprinkle with chopped parsley.

Makes 4 servings

Preparation Time: 25 minutes

Herb Roasted Turkey

1 (12-pound) turkey, thawed if frozen
$^1/_2$ cup FLEISCHMANN'S® Original Margarine, softened, divided
1 tablespoon Italian seasoning

1. Remove neck and giblets from turkey cavities. Rinse turkey; drain well and pat dry. Free legs from tucked position; do not cut band of skin. Using rubber spatula or hand, loosen skin over breast, starting at body cavity opening by legs.

2. Blend 6 tablespoons margarine and Italian seasoning. Spread 2 tablespoons herb mixture inside body cavity; spread remaining herb mixture on meat under skin. Hold skin in place at opening with wooden picks. Return legs to tucked position; turn wings back to hold neck skin in place.

3. Place turkey, breast-side up, on flat rack in shallow open pan. Insert meat thermometer deep into thickest part of thigh next to body, not touching bone. Melt remaining 2 tablespoons margarine; brush over skin.

4. Roast at 325°F for $3^1/_2$ to $3^3/_4$ hours. When skin is golden brown, shield breast loosely with foil to prevent overbrowning. Check for doneness; thigh temperature should be 180°F to 185°F. Transfer turkey to cutting board; let stand 15 to 20 minutes before carving. Remove wooden toothpicks just before carving. *Makes 12 servings*

Preparation Time: 20 minutes
Cook Time: 3 hours and 30 minutes
Cooling Time: 15 minutes
Total Time: 4 hours and 5 minutes

Chicken Tetrazzini with Roasted Red Peppers

6 ounces uncooked egg noodles

3 tablespoons butter or margarine

$^1/_4$ cup all-purpose flour

1 can (14$^1/_2$ ounces) chicken broth

1 cup whipping cream

2 tablespoons dry sherry

2 cans (6 ounces each) sliced mushrooms, drained

1 jar (7$^1/_2$ ounces) roasted red peppers, cut into $^1/_2$-inch strips

2 cups chopped cooked chicken

1 teaspoon dried Italian seasoning

$^1/_2$ cup (2 ounces) grated Parmesan cheese

1. Cook egg noodles according to package directions. Drain well.

2. While noodles are cooking, melt butter in medium saucepan over medium heat. Add flour and whisk until smooth. Add chicken broth; bring to a boil over high heat. Remove from heat. Gradually add whipping cream and sherry; stir to combine.

3. Combine mushrooms, red peppers and noodles in large bowl; toss to combine. Add half the chicken broth mixture to noodle mixture. Combine remaining chicken broth mixture, chicken and Italian seasoning in large bowl.

4. Spoon noodle mixture into serving dish. Make a well in center of noodles and spoon in chicken mixture. Sprinkle cheese over top.

Makes 6 servings

Prep and Cook Time: 20 minutes

Chicken Tetrazzini with Roasted Red Peppers

Buttermilk Ranch Fried Chicken

2$^1/_2$ to 3 pounds frying chicken pieces
    WESSON® Vegetable Oil
2$^1/_4$ cups all-purpose flour
1$^1/_4$ tablespoons dried dill weed
1$^1/_2$ teaspoons salt
  $^3/_4$ teaspoon pepper
2$^1/_2$ cups buttermilk

Rinse chicken and pat dry; set aside. Fill a large deep-fry pot or electric skillet to no more than half its depth with Wesson® Oil. Heat oil to 325°F to 350°F. In a medium bowl, combine flour, dill, salt and pepper. Fill another bowl with buttermilk. Place chicken, one piece at a time, in buttermilk; shake off excess liquid. Coat lightly in flour mixture; shake off excess flour. Dip once again in buttermilk and flour mixture. Fry chicken, a few pieces at a time, skin side down, for 10 to 14 minutes. Turn chicken and fry 12 to 15 minutes longer or until juices run clear; drain on paper towels. Let stand 7 minutes before serving. *Makes 4 to 6 servings*

Tip: To reduce frying time by 7 to 9 minutes per side, simply cook unbreaded chicken in boiling water for 15 minutes; remove and cool completely before proceeding with recipe.

Buttermilk Ranch Fried Chicken

Campbell's® Turkey Stuffing Divan

1¼ cups boiling water

4 tablespoons margarine or butter, melted

4 cups PEPPERIDGE FARM® Herb Seasoned Stuffing

2 cups cooked broccoli cuts

2 cups cubed cooked turkey

1 can (10¾ ounces) CAMPBELL'S® Condensed Cream of Celery
    Soup *or* 98% Fat Free Cream of Celery Soup

½ cup milk

1 cup shredded Cheddar cheese (4 ounces)

1. Mix water and margarine. Add stuffing. Mix lightly.

2. Spoon into 2-quart shallow baking dish. Arrange broccoli and turkey over stuffing. In small bowl mix soup, milk and *½ cup* cheese. Pour over broccoli and turkey. Sprinkle remaining cheese over soup mixture.

3. Bake at 350°F. for 30 minutes or until hot.   *Makes 6 servings*

Variation: Substitute 1 can (10¾ ounces) CAMPBELL'S® Condensed Cream of Chicken Soup *or* 98% Fat Free Cream of Chicken Soup for Cream of Celery Soup. Substitute 2 cups cubed cooked chicken for turkey.

Tip: For 2 cups cooked broccoli cuts use about 1 pound fresh broccoli, trimmed, cut into 1-inch pieces (about 2 cups) *or* 1 package (10 ounces) frozen broccoli cuts (2 cups).

Prep Time: 15 minutes
Cook Time: 30 minutes

Campbell's® Turkey Stuffing Divan

Classic Chicken Parmesan

6 boneless, skinless chicken breast halves, pounded thin (about
   1 1/2 pounds)
2 eggs, slightly beaten
1 cup Italian seasoned dry bread crumbs
2 tablespoons olive or vegetable oil
1 jar (26 to 28 ounces) RAGÚ® Old World Style® Pasta Sauce
1 cup shredded mozzarella cheese (about 4 ounces)

Preheat oven to 375°F. Dip chicken in eggs, then bread crumbs, coating
well.

In 12-inch skillet, heat oil over medium-high heat and brown chicken;
drain on paper towels.

In 11×7-inch baking dish, evenly spread 1 cup Ragú® Old World Style
Pasta Sauce. Arrange chicken in dish, then top with remaining sauce.
Sprinkle with mozzarella cheese and, if desired, grated Parmesan cheese.
Bake 25 minutes or until chicken is no longer pink.

Makes 6 servings

Recipe Tip: To pound chicken, place a boneless, skinless breast between
two sheets of waxed paper. Use a rolling pin to press down and out from
the center to flatten.

Green Bean & Turkey Bake

1 can (10³/₄ ounces) condensed cream of mushroom soup
³/₄ cup milk
2 packages (9 ounces *each*) frozen cut green beans, thawed
2 cups (12 ounces) cubed cooked turkey or chicken
1¹/₃ cups *French's*® *Taste Toppers*™ French Fried Onions, divided
1¹/₂ cups (6 ounces) shredded Cheddar cheese, divided
3 cups hot mashed potatoes

1. Preheat oven to 375°F. In 3-quart casserole, combine soup, milk and *¹/₈ teaspoon pepper;* mix well. Stir in beans, turkey, *²/₃ cup* **Taste Toppers** and *1 cup* cheese. Spoon mashed potatoes on top.

2. Bake, uncovered, 45 minutes or until hot. Sprinkle with remaining *¹/₂ cup* cheese and *²/₃ cup* **Taste Toppers**. Bake 3 minutes or until **Taste Toppers** are golden.   *Makes 6 servings*

Microwave Directions: Prepare mixture as above except do not top with potatoes. Cover casserole with vented plastic wrap. Microwave on HIGH 15 minutes or until heated through, stirring halfway. Uncover. Top with mashed potatoes, remaining cheese and onions. Microwave on HIGH 2 to 4 minutes. Let stand 5 minutes.

Tip: Two (14¹/₂-ounce) cans cut green beans (drained) may be used instead of frozen beans. You may substitute instant mashed potatoes prepared according to package directions for 6 servings.

Prep Time: 10 minutes
Cook Time: 50 minutes

Lemon-Garlic Chicken & Rice

4 skinless, boneless chicken breast halves

1 teaspoon paprika

   Salt and pepper (optional)

2 tablespoons margarine or butter

2 cloves garlic, minced

1 package (6.9 ounces) RICE-A-RONI® Chicken Flavor

1 tablespoon lemon juice

1 cup chopped red or green bell pepper

$^1/_2$ teaspoon grated lemon peel

1. Sprinkle chicken with paprika, salt and pepper.

2. In large skillet, melt margarine over medium-high heat. Add chicken and garlic; cook 2 minutes on each side or until browned. Remove from skillet; set aside, reserving drippings. Keep warm.

3. In same skillet, sauté rice-vermicelli mix in reserved drippings over medium heat until vermicelli is golden brown. Stir in $2^1/_4$ cups water, lemon juice and Special Seasonings. Top rice with chicken; bring to a boil over high heat.

4. Cover; reduce heat. Simmer 10 minutes. Stir in red pepper and lemon peel.

5. Cover; continue to simmer 10 minutes or until liquid is absorbed, rice is tender and chicken is no longer pink inside.   *Makes 4 servings*

Lemon-Garlic Chicken & Rice

Savory Chicken with Mushrooms & Spinach

2 tablespoons margarine or butter
1 pound boneless skinless chicken breast halves, pounded thin
1 1/2 cups sliced fresh or canned mushrooms
1 package (10 ounces) fresh spinach, rinsed and drained*
1 envelope LIPTON® RECIPE SECRETS® Savory Herb with
    Garlic Soup Mix**
1 1/4 cups water

*Substitution: Use 1 package (10 ounces) frozen leaf spinach, thawed and squeezed dry.

**Also terrific with LIPTON® RECIPE SECRETS® Golden Onion Soup Mix.

1. In 12-inch skillet, heat 1 tablespoon margarine over medium-high heat and cook chicken until no longer pink; remove and keep warm.

2. In same skillet, heat remaining 1 tablespoon margarine over medium heat and cook mushrooms, stirring frequently, 2 minutes. Add spinach and cook, stirring occasionally, 3 minutes.

3. Stir in savory herb with garlic soup mix blended with water. Bring to a boil over high heat; continue boiling, stirring occasionally, 5 minutes or until sauce is thickened.

4. To serve, arrange chicken over vegetable mixture. Serve, if desired, with hot cooked rice. *Makes 4 servings*

Savory Chicken with Mushrooms & Spinach

California Chicken Pot Pies

1 (9-inch) folded refrigerated unbaked pie crust

1 can (10³/₄ ounces) cream of chicken soup

1 cup half 'n' half or milk

2 cups (10 ounces) cooked chicken, cut into ¹/₂-inch cubes

1 bag (16 ounces) California-style frozen vegetable combination,
    such as cauliflower, carrots and asparagus, thawed and drained*

1¹/₃ cups *French's*® *Taste Toppers*™ French Fried Onions, divided

¹/₄ teaspoon dried thyme leaves

¹/₂ cup (2 ounces) shredded Swiss cheese

Or, substitute any package of combination vegetables for California-style vegetables.

Preheat oven to 400°F. Roll out pie crust onto lightly floured board. Invert 10-ounce custard cup on top of crust. With sharp knife, trace around cup and cut out circle; prick several times with fork. Repeat 5 more times, rerolling scraps of pie crust as necessary. Cover; set crusts aside.

Combine soup and half 'n' half in large bowl. Stir in chicken, vegetables, ²/₃ cup **Taste Toppers** and thyme. Spoon mixture evenly into 6 (10-ounce) custard cups. Place filled cups on baking sheet. Place 1 crust over each cup. Bake, uncovered, 30 minutes or until crust is browned.

Sprinkle crusts with cheese; top with remaining ²/₃ cup **Taste Toppers**. Bake 1 minute or until **Taste Toppers** are golden.   *Makes 6 servings*

Note: Filling may be baked in 9-inch pie plate. Top with uncut 9-inch pie crust. Bake at 400°F 35 minutes or until crust is golden. Top with cheese and remaining ²/₃ cup onions. Bake 1 minute or until onions are golden.

California Chicken Pot Pies

Prepare-Ahead Tips: Pot pies may be prepared ahead, baked and frozen. Do not top with cheese and remaining onions before freezing. To reheat: Microwave individual pies in microwavable dishes on HIGH 5 minutes or until heated through. Top with remaining cheese and ²/₃ cup onions. Microwave 1 minute or until onions are golden. OR prepare pies as above. Do not bake. Cover; freeze. Bake at 400°F 40 minutes or until heated through and crust is golden. Top with cheese and remaining ²/₃ cup onions. Bake 1 minute.

Prep Time: 15 minutes
Cook Time: 31 minutes

Meaty Main Dishes

When your busy weeknights are filled with frozen dinners and take-out food, you need the weekends to slow down and relax. Sunday supper is the perfect time for simple, hearty dishes like pot roast, pork chops or corned beef and cabbage.

Roast Pork Chops with Apples and Cabbage

3 teaspoons olive oil, divided

$^{1}/_{2}$ medium onion, thinly sliced

1 teaspoon dried thyme leaves

2 cloves garlic, minced

4 pork chops, 1 inch thick (6 to 8 ounces each)

$^{1}/_{4}$ cup cider vinegar

1 tablespoon packed brown sugar

$^{1}/_{4}$ teaspoon black pepper

1 large McIntosh apple, chopped

$^{1}/_{2}$ (8-ounce) package preshredded coleslaw mix

1. Preheat oven to 375°F. Heat 2 teaspoons oil in large ovenproof skillet over medium-high heat until hot. Add onion; cover and cook 4 to 6 minutes or until onion is tender, stirring often. Add thyme and garlic; stir 30 seconds. Transfer to small bowl.

2. Add remaining 1 teaspoon oil to skillet. Sprinkle pork chops with salt and pepper. Place in skillet; cook 2 minutes per side or until browned. Transfer pork chops to plate.

3. Remove skillet from heat. Add vinegar, sugar and pepper; stir to dissolve sugar, and scrape cooked bits from skillet. Add onion mixture, apple and cabbage; cook and stir over medium-high heat until mixture is blended and liquid comes to a boil.

4. Lay pork chops on top of cabbage mixture, overlapping to fit. Cover pan and bake 15 minutes or until pork chops are juicy and just barely pink in center.

Makes 4 servings

Stuffed Green Peppers

6 medium to large green bell peppers

1 pound BOB EVANS® Original Recipe Roll Sausage

2 cups tomato sauce

2 cups water

1 small onion, chopped

1 cup uncooked rice

Sliced green onion (optional)

Preheat oven to 350°F. Slice off tops from peppers; scrape out centers to remove seeds and membranes. Combine all remaining ingredients except green onion in medium bowl; mix well. Evenly stuff peppers with sausage mixture. Place in lightly greased deep 3-quart casserole dish. Bake, covered, 20 minutes. Uncover; bake 5 to 10 minutes more or until peppers are fork-tender and filling is set. Garnish with green onion, if desired. Serve hot. Refrigerate leftovers.   *Makes 6 servings*

Tip: For a pretty presentation, slice 6 small peppers lengthwise in half through stems; scrape out centers to remove seeds and membranes. Proceed as directed, serving 2 halves to each guest.

Serve with mixed salad of carrot, radish and cucumber slices drizzled with a vinaigrette.

Stuffed Green Pepper

Peppered Pork Tenderloin

    1 pork tenderloin, about one pound

    2 teaspoons lemon pepper

    $^1/_2$ teaspoon cayenne (red pepper) OR pepper blend seasoning

Rub tenderloin all over with combined peppers; place in shallow roasting pan and roast in 425°F oven for 15 to 20 minutes, until internal temperature (measured with a meat thermometer) reads 155° to 160°F. Let roast rest for 5 minutes before slicing. *Makes 4 servings*

Favorite recipe from **National Pork Producers Council**

Onion-Baked Pork Chops

1 envelope LIPTON® RECIPE SECRETS® Golden Onion Soup
   Mix*
$^{1}/_{3}$ cup plain dry bread crumbs
4 pork chops, 1 inch thick (about 3 pounds)
1 egg, well beaten

*Also terrific with LIPTON® RECIPE SECRETS® Onion, Savory Herb with Garlic or Fiesta Herb with Red Pepper Soup Mix.

1. Preheat oven to 400°F. In small bowl, combine soup mix and bread crumbs. Dip chops in egg, then bread crumb mixture, until evenly coated.

2. In lightly greased 13×9-inch baking or roasting pan, arrange chops.

3. Bake uncovered 20 minutes or until done, turning once.

Makes 4 servings

In addition to a green vegetable, serve these pork chops with Garlic Mashed Potatoes (page 70) or with Golden Apples and Yams (page 82), for a nice change of pace.

Onion-Baked Pork Chop

Beef Tenderloins in Wild Mushroom Sauce

2 boxes UNCLE BEN'S® Butter & Herb Long Grain & Wild Rice

4 bacon slices, cut into 1-inch pieces

4 beef tenderloin steaks (4 ounces each) *or* 1 pound beef top
    sirloin steak, cut into 4 pieces

1 package (4 ounces) sliced mixed exotic mushrooms
    (crimini, shiitake and oyster) or button mushrooms

1 cup chopped onion

2/3 cup half-and-half

2 tablespoons Dijon mustard

2 tablespoons Worcestershire sauce

1. Prepare rice according to package directions.

2. Meanwhile, cook bacon over medium-high heat in large skillet until crisp; remove bacon from skillet, reserving 1 tablespoon drippings. Drain bacon on paper towels; set aside.

3. Add steaks to drippings in skillet; cook 2 minutes on each side or until browned. Reduce heat to medium; continue to cook steaks 3 to 4 minutes on each side for medium-rare or to desired doneness. Remove steaks from skillet, reserving drippings in skillet; cover steaks to keep warm.

4. Add mushrooms and onion to drippings in skillet; cook and stir over medium heat until tender, about 5 minutes, stirring occasionally.

5. In small bowl, combine half-and-half, mustard and Worcestershire sauce; mix well. Add to skillet with bacon; cook 3 minutes or until sauce thickens, stirring occasionally.

6. Return steaks to skillet. Continue to cook 3 minutes or until hot, turning steaks over once.

7. Season with salt and pepper to taste, if desired. Transfer steaks to serving plates; top with sauce. Serve with rice.   *Makes 4 servings*

Hunt's® Homestyle Meatloaf

1¹/₂ pounds ground beef

12 ounces pork sausage, casings removed

1 (8-ounce) can HUNT'S® Tomato Sauce, divided

1 cup finely chopped onion

³/₄ cup fine dry bread crumbs

¹/₂ cup finely chopped celery

1 egg

1¹/₂ teaspoon garlic salt

¹/₂ teaspoon each rubbed sage and black pepper

¹/₂ cup HUNT'S® Tomato Ketchup

In large bowl, combine ground beef, sausage, ¹/₂ can tomato sauce, onion, bread crumbs, celery, egg, garlic salt and sage until well blended. Place mixture in shallow baking pan; form into loaf. Bake, uncovered, at 375°F for 1 hour 15 minutes; drain. Meanwhile, in small bowl, stir together remaining tomato sauce and ketchup. Spoon over loaf, coating well. Bake 15 minutes longer. Serve immediately.   *Makes 8 servings*

Spaghetti Bake

1 pound BOB EVANS® Dinner Link Sausage (regular or Italian)

1 (8-ounce) can tomato sauce

1 (6-ounce) can tomato paste

1 (4-ounce) can sliced mushrooms, drained

$1/2$ teaspoon salt

$1/2$ teaspoon dried basil leaves

$1/2$ teaspoon dried oregano leaves

6 ounces spaghetti, cooked according to package directions and drained

$1/3$ cup shredded mozzarella cheese

2 tablespoons grated Parmesan cheese

Fresh basil leaves and tomato slices (optional)

Preheat oven to 375°F. Cut sausage links into bite-size pieces. Cook in medium skillet over medium heat until browned, stirring occasionally. Drain off any drippings; set sausage aside. Combine tomato sauce, tomato paste, mushrooms, salt, dried basil and oregano in large bowl. Add spaghetti and reserved sausage; mix well. Spoon into lightly greased $1^{1}/2$-quart casserole dish; sprinkle with cheeses. Bake 20 to 30 minutes or until heated through. Garnish with fresh basil and tomato slices, if desired. Serve hot. Refrigerate leftovers. *Makes 4 servings*

Spaghetti Bake

Corned Beef and Cabbage with Parsley Dumplings

1 (4-pound) corned beef brisket, rinsed and trimmed
2 tablespoons TABASCO® brand Green Pepper Sauce
1 small green cabbage, coarsely shredded

PARSLEY DUMPLINGS
2 cups flour
1 tablespoon baking powder
$^1/_4$ teaspoon salt
1 cup milk
1 egg, beaten
2 tablespoons chopped fresh parsley
1 tablespoon butter *or* margarine, melted
2 teaspoons TABASCO® brand Green Pepper Sauce

Place corned beef in large saucepan with enough cold water to cover by
2 inches; add TABASCO® Green Pepper Sauce. Heat to boiling over high
heat. Reduce heat to low; cover and simmer 2 hours, occasionally
skimming surface.

During last 10 minutes of cooking corned beef, add cabbage to cooking
liquid; return to boil over high heat. Reduce heat, cover and simmer
10 minutes or until cabbage is tender. Remove corned beef and cabbage
to warm serving platter; keep warm. Reserve liquid in saucepan.

For Parsley Dumplings, combine flour, baking powder and salt in large
bowl. Whisk milk, egg, parsley, butter and TABASCO® Green Pepper
Sauce in small bowl until blended. Stir milk mixture into dry ingredients

Corned Beef and Cabbage with Parsley Dumplings

just until blended. Form dumplings by dropping tablespoonfuls of batter into reserved simmering liquid. Cover and simmer 10 minutes or until dumplings are cooked in center. Transfer dumplings to platter with corned beef and cabbage using slotted spoon. *Makes 6 to 8 servings*

Mustard-Crusted Roast Pork

3 tablespoons Dijon mustard

4 teaspoons minced garlic, divided

2 whole well-trimmed pork tenderloins (about 1 pound each)

2 tablespoons dried thyme leaves

1 teaspoon black pepper

$1/2$ teaspoon salt

1 pound asparagus spears, ends trimmed

2 red or yellow bell peppers (or one of each), cut into strips

1 cup fat-free reduced-sodium chicken broth, divided

1. Preheat oven to 375°F. Combine mustard and 3 teaspoons garlic in small bowl. Place tenderloins on waxed paper; spread mustard mixture over top and sides of tenderloins. Combine thyme, black pepper and salt in small bowl; reserve 1 teaspoon mixture. Sprinkle remaining mixture over tenderloins, patting so that seasoning adheres to mustard. Place tenderloins on rack in shallow roasting pan. Roast 25 minutes.

2. Arrange asparagus and bell peppers in single layer in shallow casserole or 13×9-inch baking pan. Add $1/4$ cup broth, reserved thyme mixture and remaining 1 teaspoon garlic; toss to coat.

3. Roast vegetables in oven, alongside pork tenderloins, 15 to 20 minutes or until thermometer inserted into center of pork registers 160°F and vegetables are tender. Transfer pork to carving board; tent with foil and let stand 5 minutes. Arrange vegetables on serving platter, reserving juices in dish; cover and keep warm. Add remaining $3/4$ cup broth and juices in dish to roasting pan. Place over range-top burner(s); simmer 3 to 4 minutes over medium-high heat or until reduced to $3/4$ cup, stirring frequently. Cut pork crosswise into $1/4$-inch slices; arrange on serving platter. Spoon juices over tenderloin and vegetables. *Makes 8 servings*

Mustard-Crusted Roast Pork

Yankee Pot Roast and Vegetables

1 beef chuck pot roast (2$\frac{1}{2}$ pounds)

Salt and black pepper

3 medium baking potatoes (about 1 pound), unpeeled and cut
    into quarters

2 large carrots, cut into $\frac{3}{4}$-inch slices

2 ribs celery, cut into $\frac{3}{4}$-inch slices

1 medium onion, sliced

1 large parsnip, cut into $\frac{3}{4}$-inch slices

2 bay leaves

1 teaspoon dried rosemary leaves

$\frac{1}{2}$ teaspoon dried thyme leaves

$\frac{1}{2}$ cup reduced-sodium beef broth

Slow Cooker Directions

1. Trim excess fat from meat and discard. Cut meat into serving pieces;
sprinkle with salt and pepper.

2. Combine vegetables, bay leaves, rosemary and thyme in slow cooker.
Place beef over vegetables. Pour broth over beef. Cover and cook on LOW
8$\frac{1}{2}$ to 9 hours or until beef is fork-tender. Remove beef to serving platter.
Arrange vegetables around beef. Remove and discard bay leaves.

Makes 10 to 12 servings

Note: To make gravy, ladle the juices into a 2-cup measure; let stand
5 minutes. Skim off and discard fat. Measure remaining juices and heat to
a boil in small saucepan. For each cup of juice, mix 2 tablespoons of flour
with $\frac{1}{4}$ cup of cold water until smooth. Stir mixture into boiling juices,
stirring constantly 1 minute or until thickened.

Herb-Crusted Roast Beef and Potatoes

1 (4$\frac{1}{2}$-pound) eye of round or sirloin tip beef roast

$\frac{3}{4}$ cup plus 2 tablespoons FILIPPO BERIO® Olive Oil, divided

    Salt and freshly ground black pepper

2 tablespoons paprika

2 pounds small red skin potatoes, cut into halves

1 cup dry bread crumbs

1 teaspoon dried thyme leaves

1 teaspoon dried rosemary

$\frac{1}{2}$ teaspoon salt

$\frac{1}{4}$ teaspoon freshly ground black pepper

Preheat oven to 325°F. Brush roast with 2 tablespoons olive oil. Season to taste with salt and pepper. Place in large roasting pan; insert meat thermometer into center of thickest part of roast. Roast 45 minutes.

Meanwhile, in large bowl, combine $\frac{1}{2}$ cup olive oil and paprika. Add potatoes; toss until lightly coated. In small bowl, combine bread crumbs, thyme, rosemary, $\frac{1}{2}$ teaspoon salt, $\frac{1}{4}$ teaspoon pepper and remaining $\frac{1}{4}$ cup olive oil.

Carefully remove roast from oven. Place potatoes around roast. Press bread crumb mixture onto top of roast to form crust. Sprinkle any remaining bread crumb mixture over potatoes. Roast an additional 40 to 45 minutes or until meat thermometer registers 145°F for medium-rare or until desired doneness is reached. Transfer roast to carving board; tent with foil. Let stand 5 to 10 minutes before carving. Cut into $\frac{1}{4}$-inch-thick slices. Serve immediately with potatoes, spooning any bread crumb mixture from roasting pan onto meat. *Makes 8 servings*

Carolina Baked Beans & Pork Chops

2 cans (16 ounces each) pork and beans
$^1/_2$ cup each chopped onion and green bell pepper
$^1/_4$ cup *French's*® Classic Yellow® Mustard
$^1/_4$ cup packed light brown sugar
2 tablespoons *French's*® Worcestershire Sauce
1 tablespoon *Frank's*® *RedHot*® Sauce
6 boneless pork chops (1 inch thick)

1. Preheat oven to 400°F. Combine all ingredients *except pork chops* in 3-quart shallow baking dish; mix well. Arrange chops on top, turning once to coat with sauce.

2. Bake, uncovered, 30 to 35 minutes or until pork is no longer pink in center. Stir beans around chops once during baking. Serve with green beans or mashed potatoes, if desired.   *Makes 6 servings*

Prep Time: 10 minutes
Cook Time: 30 minutes

*For the best results with pork dishes, always
purchase pork chops that are at least 1 inch thick.
It's difficult to prevent thinner pork chops from
drying out, even with short cooking times.*

Carolina Baked Beans & Pork Chop

Country Skillet Hash

2 tablespoons butter or margarine

4 pork chops (³/₄ inch thick), diced

¹/₄ teaspoon black pepper

¹/₄ teaspoon cayenne pepper (optional)

1 medium onion, chopped

2 cloves garlic, minced

1 can (14¹/₂ ounces) DEL MONTE® Whole New Potatoes, drained and diced

1 can (14¹/₂ ounces) DEL MONTE® Diced Tomatoes, undrained

1 medium green bell pepper, chopped

¹/₂ teaspoon thyme, crushed

1. Melt butter in large skillet over medium heat. Add meat; cook, stirring occasionally, until no longer pink in center. Season with black pepper and cayenne pepper, if desired.

2. Add onion and garlic; cook until tender. Stir in potatoes, tomatoes, green pepper and thyme. Cook 5 minutes, stirring frequently. Season with salt, if desired.   *Makes 4 servings*

Tip: The hash may be topped with a poached or fried egg.

Prep Time: 10 minutes
Cook Time: 15 minutes

Country Skillet Hash

Classic Vegetables & Sides

No meal is complete without a side dish or two. Mashed potatoes, spinach salad and roasted vegetables are just a few possiblities—the only problem is choosing which recipe to make!

Roasted Mixed Vegetables

4 large red skin potatoes, cut into wedges (about 2 pounds)

3 large carrots, peeled and cut into $1^{1}/_{2}$-inch pieces (about 2 cups)

3 large parsnips, peeled and cut into $1^{1}/_{2}$-inch pieces (about 2 cups)

2 large onions, cut into wedges

1 tablespoon dried rosemary leaves

2 teaspoons garlic powder

$^{1}/_{4}$ cup FLEISCHMANN'S® Original Margarine, melted

1. Mix potatoes, carrots, parsnips and onions with rosemary and garlic powder in large bowl.

2. Drizzle with melted margarine, tossing to coat well. Spread vegetables in 13×9×2-inch baking pan.

3. Bake at 450°F for 40 to 45 minutes or until fork-tender, stirring occasionally.   *Makes 8 servings*

Preparation Time: 15 minutes
Cook Time: 40 minutes
Total Time: 55 minutes

Baked Spinach Risotto

1 tablespoon olive oil

1 green bell pepper, chopped

1 medium onion, chopped

2 cloves garlic, minced

1 cup arborio rice

3 cups chopped fresh spinach leaves

1 (14^1/$_2$-ounce) can chicken broth

^{1}/$_2$ cup grated Parmesan cheese, divided

1 tablespoon TABASCO® brand Green Pepper Sauce

1 teaspoon salt

Preheat oven to 400°F. Grease 1^1/$_2$-quart casserole. Heat oil in 10-inch skillet over medium heat. Add green bell pepper, onion and garlic; cook 5 minutes. Add rice; stir to coat well. Stir in spinach, chicken broth, ^{1}/$_4$ cup Parmesan cheese, TABASCO® Green Pepper Sauce and salt. Spoon mixture into prepared baking dish. Sprinkle with remaining ^{1}/$_4$ cup Parmesan cheese. Bake 35 to 40 minutes or until rice is tender.

Makes 4 servings

Arborio is a translucent, short-grain Italian rice that is very high in starch. It is traditionally used to make risotto because it produces the characteristic creamy texture.

Baked Spinach Risotto

Mediterranean Greek Salad

$^1/_2$ cup olive oil

$^1/_3$ cup red wine vinegar

2 teaspoons chopped fresh oregano *or* $^3/_4$ teaspoon dried oregano

1 teaspoon LAWRY'S® Seasoned Salt

1 teaspoon LAWRY'S® Garlic Powder with Parsley

3 medium cucumbers, peeled and chopped

3 to 4 medium tomatoes, seeded and coarsely chopped

1 medium onion, thinly sliced and separated into rings

1 can (6 ounces) Greek or ripe olives, drained, pitted

1 cup (4 ounces) crumbled feta cheese

In container with stopper or lid, combine oil, vinegar, oregano and seasonings. Cover; shake well. Set dressing aside. In medium bowl, combine cucumbers, tomatoes, onion, olives and cheese; mix lightly. Shake dressing. Add to salad; toss lightly to coat. Refrigerate 30 minutes.

Makes 8 servings

Serving Suggestion: Serve with heated pita bread and spread with herb-flavored butter.

Hint: Substitute a Lawry's® classic dressing such as Caesar or Red Wine Vinaigrette for first 5 ingredients.

Mediterranean Greek Salad

Garlic Mashed Potatoes

6 medium all-purpose potatoes, peeled, if desired, and cut into
　　chunks (about 3 pounds)
　Water
1 envelope LIPTON® RECIPE SECRETS® Garlic Mushroom
　　Soup Mix*
1/2 cup milk
1/2 cup margarine or butter

Also terrific with LIPTON® RECIPE SECRETS® Savory Herb with Garlic, Onion-Mushroom, Onion or Golden Onion Soup Mix.

In 4-quart saucepan, cover potatoes with water; bring to a boil over high heat.

Reduce heat to low and simmer, uncovered, 20 minutes or until potatoes are very tender; drain.

Return potatoes to saucepan, then mash. Stir in remaining ingredients.

Makes about 8 servings

Ginger Fruit Salad

1/3 cup HELLMANN'S® or BEST FOODS® Real, Light or Low
    Fat Mayonnaise Dressing
2 tablespoons orange juice
1/8 teaspoon ground ginger
2 medium oranges, sectioned
1 kiwifruit, peeled and sliced
1 cup fresh raspberries
    Sliced star fruit for garnish (optional)
    Pomegranate seeds for garnish (optional)

1. In medium bowl combine mayonnaise, orange juice and ginger.

2. Arrange orange sections, kiwi slices and raspberries on 4 serving plates. Spoon dressing over fruit. Garnish with sliced star fruit and pomegranate seeds, if desired. *Makes 4 servings*

*Choose pomegranates that are firm and heavy
with a rich, even red color. You might want to wear
rubber gloves and an apron while handling them, as
the juice can squirt and splatter when the seeds pop
open, staining both skin and clothing.*

Honey Nut Squash

2 acorn squash (about 6 ounces each)

¼ cup honey

2 tablespoons butter or margarine, melted

2 tablespoons chopped walnuts

2 tablespoons raisins

2 teaspoons Worcestershire sauce

Cut acorn squash lengthwise into halves; do not remove seeds. Place cut sides up in baking pan or on baking sheet. Bake at 400°F 30 to 45 minutes or until soft. Remove seeds and fibers.

Combine honey, butter, walnuts, raisins and Worcestershire sauce; spoon into squash. Bake 5 to 10 minutes more or until lightly glazed.

Makes 4 servings

Microwave Directions: Cut acorn squash lengthwise into halves and remove seeds. Microwave according to manufacturer's directions. Combine honey, butter, walnuts, raisins and Worcestershire sauce; spoon into squash. Microwave at HIGH (100%) 30 seconds or until thoroughly heated and lightly glazed.

Favorite recipe from **National Honey Board**

Honey Nut Squash

Roasted Idaho & Sweet Potatoes

1 envelope LIPTON® RECIPE SECRETS® Onion Soup Mix
2 medium all-purpose potatoes, peeled, if desired, and cut into
  large chunks (about 1 pound)
2 medium sweet potatoes or yams, peeled, if desired, and cut into
  large chunks (about 1 pound)
1/4 cup olive or vegetable oil

1. Preheat oven to 425°F. In large plastic bag or bowl, add all ingredients. Close bag and shake, or toss in bowl, until potatoes are evenly coated.

2. In 13×9-inch baking or roasting pan, arrange potatoes; discard bag.

3. Bake uncovered, stirring occasionally, 40 minutes or until potatoes are tender and golden.   *Makes 4 servings*

Ultimate Macaroni & Cheese

2 cups (8 ounces) elbow macaroni, uncooked
1 pound (16 ounces) VELVEETA® Pasteurized Prepared Cheese
  Product, cut up
1/2 cup milk
  Dash pepper

1. Cook macaroni as directed on package; drain well. Return to same pan.

2. Add Velveeta, milk and pepper to same pan. Stir on low heat until Velveeta is melted. Serve immediately.   *Makes 4 to 6 servings*

Prep Time: 5 minutes
Cook Time: 15 minutes

Roasted Idaho & Sweet Potatoes

Pepperidge Farm® Scalloped Apple Bake

$^{1}/_{4}$ cup margarine *or* butter, melted

$^{1}/_{4}$ cup sugar

2 teaspoons grated orange peel

1 teaspoon ground cinnamon

1 $^{1}/_{2}$ cups PEPPERIDGE FARM® Corn Bread Stuffing

$^{1}/_{2}$ cup coarsely chopped pecans

1 can (16 ounces) whole berry cranberry sauce

$^{1}/_{3}$ cup orange juice *or* water

4 large cooking apples, cored and thinly sliced (about 6 cups)

1. Lightly mix margarine, sugar, orange peel, cinnamon, stuffing and pecans and set aside.

2. Mix cranberry sauce, juice and apples. Add *half* the stuffing mixture. Mix lightly. Spoon into 8-inch square baking dish. Sprinkle remaining stuffing mixture over apple mixture.

3. Bake at 375°F. for 40 minutes or until apples are tender.

Makes 6 servings

Tip: To melt margarine, remove wrapper and place margarine in microwave-safe cup. Cover and microwave on HIGH 45 seconds.

Prep Time: 25 minutes
Cook Time: 40 minutes

Classic Spinach Salad

$^1/_2$ pound fresh spinach leaves (about 10 cups)
1 cup sliced mushrooms
1 medium tomato, cut into wedges
$^1/_3$ cup seasoned croutons
$^1/_4$ cup chopped red onion
4 slices bacon, crisp-cooked and crumbled
$^1/_2$ cup WISH-BONE® Olive Oil Vinaigrette Dressing
1 hard-cooked egg, sliced

In large salad bowl, combine spinach, mushrooms, tomato, croutons, red onion and bacon. Add olive oil vinaigrette dressing and toss gently. Garnish with egg.   *Makes about 6 side-dish servings*

BelGioioso® Parmesan Polenta

Nonstick vegetable oil spray
4 cups canned vegetable broth
$1^1/_2$ cups yellow cornmeal
$^3/_4$ cup grated BELGIOIOSO® Parmesan Cheese (about 2 ounces)

Preheat oven to 375°F. Spray 8×8×2-inch glass baking dish with vegetable oil spray. Bring vegetable broth to a boil in medium heavy saucepan over medium heat. Gradually whisk in cornmeal. Continue to whisk until mixture is very thick, about 3 minutes. Mix in BelGioioso Parmesan Cheese and pour mixture into prepared dish. Bake polenta until top begins to brown, about 30 minutes. Serve hot.

Makes 4 to 6 servings

Country-Style Sausage Potato Salad

3 pounds red potatoes, cut into 1-inch chunks, boiled until tender
    and drained
2 tablespoons cider vinegar, divided
1 (9-ounce) HILLSHIRE FARM® Summer Sausage, cut
    lengthwise into quarters, then sliced
2 tablespoons packed brown sugar
2 tablespoons Dijon mustard
1 tablespoon olive oil
$1/2$ teaspoon salt
$1/2$ teaspoon black pepper
$1/2$ cup sliced green onions
$1/4$ cup chopped parsley

Place warm potatoes in serving bowl; toss with 1 tablespoon vinegar. Cook
Summer Sausage in medium skillet over medium heat until nearly crisp,
about 5 minutes; drain and set aside. Combine brown sugar, mustard, oil,
remaining 1 tablespoon vinegar, salt and pepper in small bowl. Pour brown
sugar mixture, sausage, onions and parsley over potatoes; toss to mix.
Serve warm.   *Makes 10 to 12 side-dish servings*

*Their lower starch and higher moisture contents make
round red potatoes good for boiling and mashing.*

Country-Style Sausage Potato Salad

Original Ranch® Roasted Potatoes

2 pounds small red potatoes, quartered
1/4 cup vegetable oil
1 packet (1 ounce) HIDDEN VALLEY® ORIGINAL RANCH®
   Salad Dressing & Recipe Mix

Place potatoes in a resealable plastic bag and add oil; seal bag. Toss to coat. Add salad dressing & recipe mix and toss again until coated. Bake in an ungreased baking pan at 450°F. for 35 minutes or until potatoes are brown and crisp.   *Makes 4 to 6 servings*

Cherry Waldorf Salad

1 1/4 cups apple juice, divided
1 package (4-serving size) JELL-O® Brand Cherry Flavor
   Sugar Free Gelatin
Ice cubes
1/2 cup finely chopped peeled apple
1 small banana, sliced or finely chopped
1/4 cup sliced celery

BRING 3/4 cup of the apple juice to a boil in medium saucepan. Completely dissolve gelatin in boiling apple juice. Combine the remaining 1/2 cup apple juice and enough ice cubes to measure 1 1/4 cups. Add to gelatin; stir until slightly thickened. Remove any unmelted ice. Stir in fruit and celery. Spoon into individual dishes or medium serving bowl. Chill until firm, about 2 hours.   *Makes 2 1/2 cups or 5 servings*

Caesar Salad

12 cups torn romaine lettuce leaves

$^1/_2$ cup egg substitute

$^1/_4$ cup olive oil*

$^1/_4$ cup lemon juice

1 teaspoon GREY POUPON® Dijon Mustard

2 cloves garlic, minced

$^1/_4$ teaspoon ground black pepper

Grated Parmesan cheese, optional

*Vegetable oil can be substituted.

Place lettuce in large bowl; set aside.

In small bowl, whisk together egg substitute, oil, lemon juice, mustard, garlic and pepper until well blended. To serve, pour dressing over lettuce, tossing until well coated. Serve with Parmesan cheese, if desired.

Makes 8 servings

Prep Time: 15 minutes

Golden Apples and Yams

2 large yams or sweet potatoes

2 Washington Golden Delicious apples, cored and sliced crosswise
  into rings

$1/4$ cup firmly packed brown sugar

1 teaspoon cornstarch

$1/8$ teaspoon ground cloves

$1/2$ cup orange juice

2 tablespoons chopped pecans or walnuts

Heat oven to 400°F. Bake yams 50 minutes or until soft but still hold
their shape. (This can also be done in microwave.) Let yams cool enough
to handle. *Reduce oven to 350°F.*

Peel and slice yams crosswise. In shallow 1-quart baking dish, alternate
apple rings and yam slices, overlapping edges slightly. In small saucepan,
combine sugar, cornstarch and cloves; stir in orange juice and mix well.
Heat orange juice mixture over medium heat, stirring, until thickened;
pour over apples and yams. Sprinkle with nuts; bake 20 minutes or until
apples and yams are tender.   *Makes 6 servings*

Favorite recipe from **Washington Apple Commission**

Golden Apples and Yams

Old-Fashioned Cakes & Cookies

*What would Sunday supper be without
a beautiful layer cake or a batch of
fresh-baked cookies to look forward to?
Here are some delicious ways to end the
evening on a sweet note.*

Cheesecake Classic

1 (8-ounce) package cream cheese

$^1/_2$ cup plus 2 tablespoons sugar, divided

1 tablespoon lemon juice

$^1/_2$ teaspoon vanilla, divided

Dash salt

2 eggs

1 (6-ounce) READY CRUST® Graham Cracker Pie Crust

1 cup sour cream

Fresh fruit for garnish

1. Preheat oven to 325°F. Combine cream cheese, $^1/_2$ cup sugar, lemon juice, $^1/_4$ teaspoon vanilla and salt in medium bowl. Mix until well blended. Add eggs, 1 at a time, mixing well after each addition.

2. Place crust on baking sheet. Pour cream cheese mixture into crust. Bake 25 to 30 minutes or until knife inserted near center comes out clean.

3. Combine sour cream, remaining 2 tablespoons sugar and $^1/_4$ teaspoon vanilla in small bowl. Carefully spread over cake. Bake 10 minutes; cool on wire rack. Chill 3 hours. Top with fresh fruit. Refrigerate leftovers.

Makes 8 servings

Preparation Time: 10 minutes

Baking Time: 35 to 40 minutes

Chilling Time: 3 hours

Celebration Pumpkin Cake

   1 package (18 ounces) spice cake mix
   1 can (16 ounces) solid-pack pumpkin
   3 eggs
   1/4 cup butter, softened
   1 1/2 containers (16 ounces each) cream cheese frosting
   1/3 cup caramel topping
      Pecan halves

Preheat oven to 350°F. Grease and flour 3 (9-inch) round cake pans. Combine cake mix, pumpkin, eggs and butter in large bowl; beat with electric mixer at medium speed 2 minutes. Divide batter evenly among prepared pans. Bake 20 to 25 minutes or until toothpick inserted in centers comes out clean. Cool 5 minutes on wire racks; remove from pans and cool completely.

Place one cake layer on serving plate; cover with frosting. Repeat layers, ending with frosting. Frost side of cake. Spread caramel topping over top of cake, letting some caramel drip down side. Garnish with pecan halves.

Makes 16 servings

*For the best results when baking, arrange cake
pans so there are at least 2 inches between each
other and the sides of the oven.*

Celebration Pumpkin Cake

Chewy Oatmeal Cookies

¾ Butter Flavor* CRISCO® Stick or ¾ cup Butter Flavor
    CRISCO® all-vegetable shortening, plus additional for
    greasing
1¼ cups firmly packed light brown sugar
  1 egg
⅓ cup milk
1½ teaspoons vanilla
  3 cups quick cooking oats, uncooked
  1 cup all-purpose flour
½ teaspoon baking soda
½ teaspoon salt
¼ teaspoon ground cinnamon
  1 cup raisins
  1 cup coarsely chopped walnuts

Butter Flavor Crisco is artificially flavored.

1. Heat oven to 375°F. Grease baking sheets with shortening. Place sheets of foil on countertop for cooling cookies.

2. Combine ¾ cup shortening, brown sugar, egg, milk and vanilla in large bowl. Beat at medium speed of electric mixer until well blended.

3. Combine oats, flour, baking soda, salt and cinnamon. Mix into creamed mixture at low speed just until blended. Stir in raisins and nuts.

4. Drop rounded tablespoonfuls of dough 2 inches apart onto prepared baking sheet. Bake one baking sheet at a time at 375°F for 10 to 12 minutes, or until lightly browned. *Do not overbake.* Cool 2 minutes on baking sheet. Remove cookies to foil to cool completely.

Makes about 2½ dozen cookies

Chewy Oatmeal Cookies

Mississippi Nilla Mud Cake

1 1/2 cups margarine or butter, divided

4 eggs

1 cup unsweetened cocoa, divided

2 cups sugar

1 1/2 cups all-purpose flour

1 1/4 cups PLANTERS® Pecans, chopped

1/4 teaspoon salt

3 cups miniature marshmallows

35 NILLA® Wafers

1 (1-pound) package powdered sugar

1/2 cup milk

1/2 teaspoon vanilla extract

1. Preheat oven to 350°F. Beat 1 cup margarine or butter, eggs and 1/2 cup cocoa in large bowl with electric mixer at medium speed until well combined. Blend in sugar, flour, pecans and salt. Spread batter into greased 13×9×2-inch baking pan. Bake at 350°F for 30 to 35 minutes or until cake pulls away from sides of pan.

2. Sprinkle marshmallows over hot cake; return to oven for 2 minutes or until marshmallows are slightly puffed. Arrange wafers over marshmallow layer.

3. Beat remaining 1/2 cup margarine or butter, powdered sugar, remaining 1/2 cup cocoa, milk and vanilla in medium bowl with electric mixer at medium speed until smooth; spread immediately over wafer layer. Cool cake completely on wire rack. Cut into squares to serve.

Makes 24 servings

Choco Peanut Butter Dreams

1 1/2 cups firmly packed brown sugar

1 cup creamy or chunk-style peanut butter

3/4 cup (1 1/2 sticks) margarine, softened

1/3 cup water

1 egg

1 teaspoon vanilla

3 cups QUAKER® Oats (quick or old fashioned, uncooked)

1 1/2 cups all-purpose flour

1/2 teaspoon baking soda

1 1/2 cups semi-sweet chocolate pieces

4 teaspoons vegetable shortening

1/3 cup chopped peanuts (optional)

Preheat oven to 350°F. Beat brown sugar, peanut butter and margarine until fluffy. Blend in water, egg and vanilla. Add combined oats, flour and baking soda; mix well. Shape into 1-inch balls. Place on ungreased cookie sheet. Using bottom of glass dipped in sugar, press into 1/4-inch-thick circles. Bake 8 to 10 minutes or until edges are golden brown. Remove to wire rack; cool completely.

In saucepan over low heat, melt chocolate pieces and shortening, stirring until smooth.* Top each cookie with 1/2 teaspoon melted chocolate; sprinkle with chopped peanuts. Chill until set. Store tightly covered.

Makes about 6 dozen cookies

*Microwave Directions: Place chocolate pieces and shortening in microwavable bowl. Microwave at HIGH (100% power) 1 to 2 minutes, stirring after 1 minute and then every 30 seconds until smooth.

Philadelphia® 3-Step® Raspberry Swirl Cheesecake

2 packages (8 ounces each) PHILADELPHIA® Cream Cheese, softened

$^1/_2$ cup sugar

$^1/_2$ teaspoon vanilla

2 eggs

1 ready-to-use graham cracker crust (6 ounces or 9 inch)

3 tablespoons red raspberry preserves

1. MIX cream cheese, sugar and vanilla at medium speed with electric mixer until well blended. Add eggs; mix until blended.

2. POUR into crust. Dot top of cheesecake with preserves. Cut through batter with knife several times for marble effect.

3. BAKE at 350°F for 40 minutes or until center is almost set. Cool. Refrigerate 3 hours or overnight. Garnish with COOL WHIP Whipped Topping and raspberries.   *Makes 8 servings*

Peaches and Cream: Substitute $^1/_4$ cup peach preserves for red raspberry preserves.

Prep Time: 10 minutes
Bake Time: 40 minutes

Philadelphia® 3-Step® Raspberry Swirl Cheesecake

Coconut Pecan Bars

^{3}/$_4$ cup (1^1/$_2$ sticks) butter or margarine, softened, divided

1^1/$_4$ cups granulated sugar, divided

^{1}/$_2$ cup plus 3 tablespoons all-purpose flour, divided

1^1/$_2$ cups finely chopped pecans, divided

2 large eggs

1 tablespoon vanilla extract

1^3/$_4$ cups "M&M's"® Chocolate Mini Baking Bits, divided

1 cup shredded coconut

Preheat oven to 350°F. Lightly grease 13×9×2-inch baking pan; set aside. Melt ^{1}/$_4$ cup butter. In large bowl combine ^{3}/$_4$ cup sugar, ^{1}/$_2$ cup flour and ^{1}/$_2$ cup nuts; add melted butter and mix well. Press mixture onto bottom of prepared pan. Bake 10 minutes or until set; cool slightly. In large bowl cream remaining ^{1}/$_2$ cup butter and ^{1}/$_2$ cup sugar; beat in eggs and vanilla. Combine 1 cup "M&M's"® Chocolate Mini Baking Bits and remaining 3 tablespoons flour; stir into creamed mixture. Spread mixture over cooled crust. Combine coconut and remaining 1 cup nuts; sprinkle over batter. Sprinkle remaining ^{3}/$_4$ cup "M&M's"® Chocolate Mini Baking Bits over coconut and nuts; pat down lightly. Bake 25 to 30 minutes or until set. Cool completely. Cut into bars. Store in tightly covered container.

Makes 24 bars

Everyone's Favorite E-Z Lemon Cake

1 package (18¹/₄ ounces) two-layer yellow or lemon cake mix
    (without pudding mix preferred)
1 package (3.4 ounces) *instant* lemon pudding and pie filling
4 eggs
1 cup water
¹/₃ cup vegetable oil
    Grated peel and juice of 1 SUNKIST® lemon
        (3 tablespoons juice)
    E-Z Lemon Glaze (recipe follows)

In large bowl, combine cake and pudding mixes, eggs, water, oil and lemon juice with electric mixer at low speed 30 seconds. Beat at medium speed 2 minutes longer. Stir in lemon peel. Pour batter into well-greased and lightly floured Bundt® pan or 10-inch tube pan.

Bake at 350°F 50 to 60 minutes or until toothpick inserted in center comes out clean. Cool on wire rack 15 minutes. With narrow spatula or knife, loosen around tube and sides and invert onto cake plate. While still warm, pierce top all over with long two-prong fork or wooden skewer. Spread top with half of E-Z Lemon Glaze. Cool completely. Spoon remaining glaze over cake, allowing some to drizzle over sides.

Makes 16 servings

E-Z Lemon Glaze: In small bowl, combine 1 cup confectioners' sugar, juice of ¹/₂ SUNKIST® lemon (1¹/₂ tablespoons) and ¹/₂ tablespoon water.

Chocolate Raspberry Torte

1 $\frac{1}{3}$ cups all-purpose flour
1 cup sugar, divided
1 $\frac{1}{2}$ teaspoons baking powder
$\frac{1}{2}$ teaspoon salt
2 eggs, separated
1 cup ($\frac{1}{2}$ pint) cold whipping cream
$\frac{1}{2}$ teaspoon almond extract
Chocolate Filling & Frosting (page 98)
$\frac{1}{2}$ cup sliced almonds
$\frac{1}{4}$ cup seedless red raspberry preserves
Sweetened whipped topping (optional)

1. Heat oven to 350°F. Grease and flour two 8- or 9-inch round baking pans.

2. Stir together flour, $\frac{1}{2}$ cup sugar, baking powder and salt; set aside. Beat egg whites in large bowl until foamy; gradually add $\frac{1}{4}$ cup sugar, beating until stiff peaks form. Beat 1 cup whipping cream in small bowl until stiff; fold into beaten egg whites.

3. Combine egg yolks, remaining $\frac{1}{4}$ cup sugar and almond extract in clean small bowl; beat on medium speed of mixer 3 minutes until thick and lemon colored. Gently fold into whipped cream mixture. Gradually fold flour mixture into whipped cream mixture just until ingredients are blended (mixture will be thick). Divide batter evenly between prepared pans; smooth surface.

4. Bake 25 to 30 minutes or until cake springs back when touched lightly in center. Cool 5 minutes; remove from pans to wire racks. Cool completely.

continued on page 98

Chocolate Raspberry Torte

Chocolate Raspberry Torte, continued

5. Prepare Chocolate Filling & Frosting. Split each cake layer in half horizontally. Place one layer on serving plate; spread with $^2/_3$ cup filling. Sprinkle with 1 tablespoon almonds; repeat with two more layers. Top with last layer; spread with raspberry preserves. Frost side of cake with remaining filling. Garnish top edge with whipped cream, if desired. Sprinkle edge and center with remaining almonds; refrigerate until ready to serve. Cover; refrigerate leftover torte.   *Makes 16 servings*

Chocolate Filling & Frosting: Stir together $^2/_3$ cup sugar and $^1/_3$ cup HERSHEY®S Cocoa in medium bowl. Add $1^1/_2$ cups cold whipping cream and $1^1/_2$ teaspoons vanilla extract; beat until stiff. Makes about three cups.

Chocolate Scotcheroos

    1 cup light corn syrup
    1 cup sugar
    1 cup peanut butter
    6 cups KELLOGG'S® RICE KRISPIES® cereal
    1 package (6 ounces, 1 cup) semi-sweet chocolate morsels
    1 package (6 ounces, 1 cup) butterscotch morsels

1. Place corn syrup and sugar in large saucepan. Cook over medium heat, stirring frequently, until sugar dissolves and mixture begins to boil. Remove from heat. Stir in peanut butter; mix well. Add Kellogg's Rice Krispies® cereal. Stir until well coated. Press mixture into 13×9×2-inch pan coated with cooking spray. Set aside.

2. Melt chocolate and butterscotch morsels together in small saucepan over low heat, stirring constantly. Spread evenly over cereal mixture. Let

Oreo® Decadence Bars

1 (8-ounce) package OREO® Crunchies

2 tablespoons margarine or butter, melted

$^3/_4$ cup white chocolate chips

$^3/_4$ cup miniature marshmallows

$^3/_4$ cup PLANTERS® Walnuts, chopped

1 (14-ounce) can sweetened condensed milk

1. Preheat oven to 350°F. Combine crunchies and margarine or butter in small bowl. Sprinkle 1 cup crumb mixture over bottom of lightly greased 8×8×2-inch baking pan. Sprinkle with white chocolate chips, marshmallows and walnuts; top with remaining crumbs. Pour condensed milk evenly over crumbs.

2. Bake at 350°F for 30 minutes. Cool completely in pan. Cut into bars; store in airtight container.   *Makes 16 bars*

Caramel Oatmeal Chewies

1 $^3/_4$ cups quick or old-fashioned oats

1 $^3/_4$ cups all-purpose flour, divided

$^3/_4$ cup packed brown sugar

$^1/_2$ teaspoon baking soda

$^1/_4$ teaspoon salt (optional)

$^3/_4$ cup (1 $^1/_2$ sticks) butter or margarine, melted

1 cup chopped nuts

2 cups (12-ounce package) NESTLÉ® TOLL HOUSE®
    Semi-Sweet Chocolate Morsels

1 cup caramel ice-cream topping

COMBINE oats, 1 $^1/_2$ cups flour, brown sugar, baking soda and salt in
large bowl; stir to break up brown sugar. Stir in butter, mixing until well
blended. Reserve *1 cup* oat mixture; press remaining oat mixture onto
bottom of greased 13×9-inch baking pan. BAKE in preheated 350°F.
oven for 10 to 12 minutes or until light brown; cool on wire rack for
10 minutes. Sprinkle with nuts and morsels. Mix caramel topping with
remaining flour in small bowl; drizzle over morsels to within $^1/_4$ inch of
pan edges. Sprinkle with reserved oat mixture. BAKE at 350°F. for
18 to 22 minutes or until golden brown. Cool in pan on wire rack; chill
until firm.   *Makes about 2 $^1/_2$ dozen bars*

Caramel Oatmeal Chewies

Hershey's Best Loved Chocolate Cheesecake

Quick Chocolate Crumb Crust (recipe follows)
3 (8-ounce) packages cream cheese, softened
1¼ cups sugar
1 container (8 ounces) dairy sour cream
2 teaspoons vanilla extract
½ cup HERSHEY'S Cocoa
2 tablespoons all-purpose flour
3 eggs
Quick Chocolate Drizzle (recipe follows)

1. Prepare Quick Chocolate Crumb Crust. Heat oven to 450°F.

2. Beat cream cheese and sugar until blended. Add sour cream and vanilla; beat until blended. Beat in cocoa and flour. Add eggs, one at a time; beat just until blended. Pour into crust.

3. Bake 10 minutes. *Reduce oven temperature to 250°F;* continue baking 40 minutes. Remove from oven to wire rack. With knife, loosen cake from side of pan. Cool completely; remove side of pan. Prepare Quick Chocolate Drizzle; drizzle over top. Refrigerate 4 to 6 hours. Store covered in refrigerator. *Makes 12 servings*

Quick Chocolate Crumb Crust: Combine 1 cup chocolate wafer crumbs and ¼ cup (½ stick) butter or margarine; press onto bottom of 9-inch springform pan. Makes 1 (9-inch) crust.

Hershey's Best Loved Chocolate Cheesecake

Quick Chocolate Drizzle: Place ¹/₂ cup HERSHEY'S Semi-Sweet Chocolate Chips and 2 teaspoons shortening (do not use butter, margarine, spread or oil) in small microwave-safe bowl. Microwave at HIGH (100%) 30 seconds. If necessary, microwave at HIGH an additional 15 seconds at a time, stirring after each heating, just until chips are melted.

Fresh Berry Cobbler Cake

1 pint fresh berries (blueberries, blackberries, raspberries and/or strawberries)

1 cup all-purpose flour

1¼ cups sugar, divided

1 teaspoon baking powder

¼ teaspoon salt

3 tablespoons butter or margarine

½ cup milk

1 tablespoon cornstarch

1 cup cold water

Additional berries (optional)

Preheat oven to 375°F. Place 1 pint berries in 9×9-inch baking pan; set aside. Combine flour, ½ cup sugar, baking powder and salt in large bowl. Cut in butter with pastry blender or two knives until coarse crumbs form. Stir in milk. Spoon over berries. Combine remaining ¾ cup sugar and cornstarch in small bowl. Stir in water until sugar mixture dissolves; pour over berry mixture. Bake 35 to 40 minutes or until lightly browned. Serve warm or cool completely. Garnish with additional berries, if desired.

Makes 6 servings

Favorite recipe from **Bob Evans**®

Fresh Berry Cobbler Cake

Best-Loved Desserts

These homestyle treats provide the perfect finale to a wonderful meal. Choose from crisps, crumbles, puddings and pies—all great reasons to save room for dessert.

Peach Melba Bread Pudding

1 (16-ounce) can sliced peaches in juice

4 cups white bread cubes

$^1/_2$ cup seedless raisins

1$^1/_4$ cups skim milk

1 cup EGG BEATERS® Healthy Real Egg Product

$^1/_2$ cup sugar

2 tablespoons FLEISCHMANN'S® Original Margarine, melted

1 teaspoon vanilla extract

$^1/_4$ teaspoon ground cinnamon

$^1/_2$ cup seedless raspberry preserves, warmed, or raspberry syrup

1. Drain peaches, reserving $^1/_4$ cup juice; chop peaches. Mix bread cubes, chopped peaches and raisins in greased 2-quart shallow casserole; set aside.

2. Blend reserved peach juice, milk, Egg Beaters®, sugar, melted margarine, vanilla and cinnamon; pour over bread mixture.

3. Bake in preheated 350°F oven for 45 to 50 minutes or until knife inserted in center comes out clean. Serve warm topped with preserves or syrup. *Makes 8 servings*

Preparation Time: 20 minutes
Cook Time: 45 minutes
Total Time: 1 hour and 5 minutes

Pepperidge Farm® Apple Strudel

$^1/_2$ package (17$^1/_4$-ounce size) PEPPERIDGE FARM® Frozen
   Puff Pastry Sheets (1 sheet)
1 egg
1 tablespoon water
2 tablespoons sugar
1 tablespoon all-purpose flour
$^1/_4$ teaspoon ground cinnamon
2 large Granny Smith apples, peeled, cored and thinly sliced
   (about 3 cups)
2 tablespoons raisins

1. Thaw pastry sheet at room temperature 30 minutes. Preheat oven to 375°F. Mix egg and water and set aside. Mix sugar, flour and cinnamon. Add apples and raisins and toss to coat. Set aside.

2. Unfold pastry on lightly floured surface. Roll into 16- by 12-inch rectangle. With short side facing you, spoon apple mixture on bottom half of pastry to within 1 inch of edges. Starting at short side, roll up like a jelly roll. Place seam-side down on baking sheet. Tuck ends under to seal. Brush with egg mixture. Cut several 2-inch-long slits 2 inches apart on top.

3. Bake 35 minutes or until golden. Cool on baking sheet on wire rack 30 minutes. Slice and serve warm. Sprinkle with confectioners' sugar if desired. *Makes 6 servings*

Thaw Time: 30 minutes
Prep Time: 30 minutes
Cook Time: 35 minutes

Southern Peanut Pie

3 eggs

1 1/2 cups dark corn syrup

1/2 cup granulated sugar

1/4 cup butter, melted

1/2 teaspoon vanilla extract

1/4 teaspoon salt

1 1/2 cups chopped roasted peanuts

9-inch unbaked deep-dish pastry shell

Beat eggs until foamy. Add corn syrup, sugar, butter, vanilla and salt; continue to beat until thoroughly blended. Stir in peanuts. Pour into unbaked pastry shell. Bake in preheated 375°F oven 50 to 55 minutes. Serve warm or cold. Garnish with whipped cream or ice cream, if desired.

Makes 6 servings

Favorite recipe from **Texas Peanut Producers Board**

Dark corn syrup has a bolder flavor than light corn syrup; it is a mixture of corn syrup and refiners' syrup. They may be used interchangably in recipes, but the dark version adds color and a slightly stronger flavor.

Decadent Chocolate Mousse

1 1/4 cups semisweet chocolate chips, divided
2 cups chilled whipping cream, divided
5 egg yolks
1 teaspoon vanilla
1/4 cup sugar
1 1/2 teaspoons butter or margarine

1. Heat 1 cup chocolate chips in medium saucepan over low heat until melted, stirring often. Remove from heat; stir in 1/4 cup whipping cream.

2. Place egg yolks in medium bowl. Whisk about half of chocolate mixture into egg yolks; whisk egg yolk mixture back into chocolate mixture in saucepan. Cook over low heat 2 minutes, whisking constantly. Remove from heat; cool 3 to 5 minutes.

3. Beat remaining 1 3/4 cups whipping cream and vanilla to soft peaks in medium bowl. Gradually beat in sugar; continue beating until stiff peaks form. Stir about one-fourth of whipped cream into chocolate mixture; fold chocolate mixture into remaining whipped cream until completely combined.

4. Pour mousse into serving bowl or individual dessert dishes; cover and refrigerate 8 hours or until set. (Mousse may be refrigerated up to 2 days.)

5. Heat remaining 1/4 cup chocolate chips in small saucepan over very low heat until melted; stir in butter until smooth. Spoon mixture into small resealable plastic food storage bag. Cut small corner off bottom of bag with scissors. Pipe designs on waxed paper-lined plate; refrigerate 15 minutes or until firm. (Designs may be refrigerated up to 3 days.) Carefully peel waxed paper from chocolate designs; place designs on mousse before serving.

Makes 6 servings

Decadent Chocolate Mousse

Frozen Banana Split Pie

1 1/2 bananas, sliced
1 prepared graham cracker crumb crust (6 ounces)
2 cups cold milk
1 package (4-serving size) JELL-O® Vanilla or Banana Cream
    Flavor Instant Pudding & Pie Filling
1 tub (8 ounces) COOL WHIP® Whipped Topping, thawed
    Chocolate, strawberry and pineapple dessert toppings
    Additional banana slices
    Chopped nuts

ARRANGE banana slices on bottom of crust; set aside.

POUR milk into large bowl. Add pudding mix. Beat with wire whisk 1 minute. Gently stir in 2 cups of the whipped topping. Spread over banana slices.

FREEZE 6 hours or until firm. Let stand at room temperature or in refrigerator 15 minutes or until pie can be cut easily. Top with dessert toppings, remaining whipped topping, banana slices and nuts.

Makes 8 servings

Preparation Time: 15 minutes
Freezing Time: 6 hours

Frozen Banana Split Pie

Cherry Crisp

1 (21-ounce) can cherry pie filling
$^1/_2$ teaspoon almond extract
$^1/_2$ cup all-purpose flour
$^1/_2$ cup firmly packed brown sugar
1 teaspoon ground cinnamon
3 tablespoons butter or margarine, softened
$^1/_2$ cup chopped walnuts
$^1/_4$ cup flaked coconut
Ice cream or whipped cream (optional)

Pour cherry pie filling into ungreased 8×8×2-inch baking pan. Stir in almond extract.

Place flour, brown sugar and cinnamon in medium mixing bowl; mix well. Add butter; stir with fork until mixture is crumbly. Stir in walnuts and coconut. Sprinkle mixture over cherry pie filling.

Bake in preheated 350°F oven 25 minutes or until golden brown on top and filling is bubbly. Serve warm or at room temperature. If desired, top with ice cream or whipped cream.   *Makes 6 servings*

Note: This recipe can be doubled. Bake in two 8×8×2-inch baking pans or one 13×9×2-inch pan.

Favorite recipe from **Cherry Marketing Institute**

Baked Apple Crumble

APPLE LAYER

    6 cups sliced, peeled Golden Delicious *or* Rome Beauty apples
        (about 2 pounds or 6 medium)
    2 tablespoons orange *or* other fruit juice
    $3/4$ cup firmly packed light brown sugar
    $1/2$ cup all-purpose flour
    $1/2$ teaspoon cinnamon
    3 tablespoons CRISCO® Oil*

TOPPING (optional)

    $1/2$ cup vanilla lowfat yogurt, divided

Use your favorite Crisco Oil product.

1. Heat oven to 375°F. Oil 2-quart baking dish lightly.

2. Arrange apples evenly in dish. Drizzle with orange juice.

3. Combine brown sugar, flour and cinnamon in small bowl. Mix in 3 tablespoons oil until crumbly. Spoon over apples.

4. Bake at 375°F for 35 minutes or until apples are tender. *Do not overbake.* Cool slightly. Serve warm.

5. *For optional topping,* spoon one tablespoon vanilla yogurt over each serving. *Makes 8 servings*

Country Skillet Pudding

2 cups boiling water

1 cup packed brown sugar

6 tablespoons butter, softened, divided

2 teaspoons vanilla extract, divided

$1/2$ cup granulated sugar

$1/2$ cup milk

$1/8$ teaspoon salt

1 cup all-purpose flour

1 teaspoon baking powder

$1/2$ cup raisins

$1/2$ cup chopped walnuts or pecans

Whipped cream

Preheat oven to 350°F. Combine boiling water, brown sugar, 2 tablespoons butter and 1 teaspoon vanilla in 10-inch ovenproof skillet or similar size shallow casserole dish until smooth. Beat granulated sugar and remaining 4 tablespoons butter in medium bowl until creamy. Beat in milk, remaining 1 teaspoon vanilla and salt. Add combined flour and baking powder; beat until smooth. Fold in raisins and nuts. Spoon mixture by heaping tablespoons evenly onto liquid in skillet; do not stir or spread. Bake 25 minutes or until set and liquid is bubbly. Serve warm with whipped cream. Refrigerate leftovers.   *Makes 6 servings*

Favorite recipe from **Bob Evans**®

Country Skillet Pudding

Chocolate Chiffon Pie

2 (1-ounce) squares unsweetened chocolate, chopped

1 (14-ounce) can EAGLE® BRAND Sweetened Condensed Milk
(NOT evaporated milk)

1 envelope unflavored gelatin

$1/3$ cup water

$1/2$ teaspoon vanilla extract

1 cup ($1/2$ pint) whipping cream, whipped

1 (6-ounce) ready-made chocolate or graham cracker crumb pie
crust

Additional whipped cream

1. In heavy saucepan over low heat, melt chocolate with **Eagle Brand**.
Remove from heat.

2. Meanwhile, in small saucepan, sprinkle gelatin over water; let stand
1 minute. Over low heat, stir until gelatin dissolves.

3. Stir gelatin into chocolate mixture. Add vanilla. Cool to room
temperature. Fold in whipped cream. Spread into crust.

4. Chill 3 hours or until set. Garnish with additional whipped cream.
Store covered in refrigerator. *Makes 1 pie*

Prep Time: 20 minutes
Chill Time: 3 hours

Creamy Rice Pudding

1 1/2 **quarts 2% milk**

1 **cup sugar**

1/2 **cup MAHATMA® or CAROLINA® rice**

1/2 **cup raisins**

1 **teaspoon vanilla extract**

Combine milk, sugar and rice in a heavy saucepan. Bring to a gentle boil over medium heat; reduce heat to simmer and cook, uncovered, for 1 hour, stirring occasionally. (Milk should just barely simmer, with bubbles breaking only at outside edge of surface. After 1 hour, rice should be soft.)

Add raisins; increase heat to medium and cook about 30 minutes, stirring frequently, until rice has absorbed most, but not all, of milk and pudding is creamy.

Remove from heat and stir in vanilla. As pudding cools, it will thicken, but will be very creamy. Serve warm or chilled. *Makes 8 servings*

Old-Fashioned Ice Cream Sandwiches

          2 squares (1 ounce each) semisweet baking chocolate, coarsely
                chopped
     $^1/_2$ cup butter, softened
     $^1/_2$ cup sugar
          1 egg
          1 teaspoon vanilla
     $1^1/_2$ cups all-purpose flour
     $^1/_4$ teaspoon baking soda
     $^1/_4$ teaspoon salt
          Softened vanilla or mint chocolate chip ice cream*

One quart of ice cream can be softened in the microwave oven at HIGH about 20 seconds.

Place chocolate in 1-cup glass measuring cup. Microwave, uncovered, at HIGH 3 to 4 minutes or until chocolate is melted, stirring after 2 minutes; set aside.

Beat butter and sugar in large bowl until light and fluffy. Beat in egg and vanilla. Gradually beat in chocolate. Combine flour, baking soda and salt in small bowl; add to butter mixture. Form dough into two discs; wrap in plastic wrap and refrigerate until firm, at least 2 hours. (Dough may be refrigerated up to 3 days before baking.)

Preheat oven to 350°F. Grease cookie sheet. Roll each piece of dough between two sheets of waxed paper to $^1/_4$- to $^1/_8$-inch thickness. Remove top sheet of waxed paper; invert dough onto prepared cookie sheet. Score dough into 3×2-inch rectangles. *Do not cut completely through.* Cut excess scraps of dough from edges; add to second disc of dough and repeat rolling and scoring until all of dough is scored. Pierce each rectangle with fork.

Old-Fashioned Ice Cream Sandwiches

Bake 10 minutes or until set. Let cookies stand on cookie sheets
1 minute. Cut through score marks while cookies are still warm. Remove
cookies to wire racks; cool completely. Spread half of cookies with
softened ice cream; top with remaining cookies. Wrap in plastic wrap and
freeze 1 hour or up to 2 days.   *Makes about 8 ice cream sandwiches*

ACKNOWLEDGMENTS

The publisher would like to thank the companies and organizations listed below for the use of their recipes and photographs in this publication.

BelGioioso® Cheese, Inc.

Bestfoods

Bob Evans®

Butterball® Turkey Company

Campbell Soup Company

Cherry Marketing Institute

ConAgra Grocery Products Company

Del Monte Corporation

Eagle® Brand

Filippo Berio Olive Oil

Fleischmann's® Original Spread

The Golden Grain Company®

Grey Poupon® Dijon Mustard

Hershey Foods Corporation

Hillshire Farm®

The HV Company

Keebler Company

Kellogg Company

Kraft Foods, Inc.

Lawry's® Foods, Inc.

Lipton®

©Mars, Inc. 2001

McIlhenny Company (TABASCO® brand Pepper Sauce)

National Honey Board

National Pork Producers Council

Nestlé USA, Inc.

NILLA® Wafers

OREO® Chocolate Sandwich Cookies

The Procter & Gamble Company

The Quaker® Oatmeal Kitchens

Reckitt Benckiser

Riviana Foods Inc.

Sunkist Growers

Texas Peanut Producers Board

Uncle Ben's Inc.

Veg•All®

Washington Apple Commission

VOLUME MEASUREMENTS (dry)

$^1/_8$ teaspoon = 0.5 mL
$^1/_4$ teaspoon = 1 mL
$^1/_2$ teaspoon = 2 mL
$^3/_4$ teaspoon = 4 mL
1 teaspoon = 5 mL
1 tablespoon = 15 mL
2 tablespoons = 30 mL
$^1/_4$ cup = 60 mL
$^1/_3$ cup = 75 mL
$^1/_2$ cup = 125 mL
$^2/_3$ cup = 150 mL
$^3/_4$ cup = 175 mL
1 cup = 250 mL
2 cups = 1 pint = 500 mL
3 cups = 750 mL
4 cups = 1 quart = 1 L

VOLUME MEASUREMENTS (fluid)

1 fluid ounce (2 tablespoons) = 30 mL
4 fluid ounces ($^1/_2$ cup) = 125 mL
8 fluid ounces (1 cup) = 250 mL
12 fluid ounces (1$^1/_2$ cups) = 375 mL
16 fluid ounces (2 cups) = 500 mL

WEIGHTS (mass)

$^1/_2$ ounce = 15 g
1 ounce = 30 g
3 ounces = 90 g
4 ounces = 120 g
8 ounces = 225 g
10 ounces = 285 g
12 ounces = 360 g
16 ounces = 1 pound = 450 g

DIMENSIONS

$^1/_{16}$ inch = 2 mm
$^1/_8$ inch = 3 mm
$^1/_4$ inch = 6 mm
$^1/_2$ inch = 1.5 cm
$^3/_4$ inch = 2 cm
1 inch = 2.5 cm

OVEN TEMPERATURES

250°F = 120°C
275°F = 140°C
300°F = 150°C
325°F = 160°C
350°F = 180°C
375°F = 190°C
400°F = 200°C
425°F = 220°C
450°F = 230°C

BAKING PAN SIZES

Utensil	Size in Inches/Quarts	Metric Volume	Size in Centimeters
Baking or	8×8×2	2 L	20×20×5
Cake Pan	9×9×2	2.5 L	23×23×5
(square or	12×8×2	3 L	30×20×5
rectangular)	13×9×2	3.5 L	33×23×5
Loaf Pan	8×4×3	1.5 L	20×10×7
	9×5×3	2 L	23×13×7
Round Layer	8×1½	1.2 L	20×4
Cake Pan	9×1½	1.5 L	23×4
Pie Plate	8×1¼	750 mL	20×3
	9×1¼	1 L	23×3
Baking Dish	1 quart	1 L	—
or Casserole	1½ quart	1.5 L	—
	2 quart	2 L	—